# Inspiring Stories From The Great Depression For Kids

*True Tales of Resilience, Kindness, and Strength to Bring History to Life for Children*

# Welcome Aboard, Check Out This Limited-Time Free Bonus!

Ahoy, reader! Welcome to the Ahoy Publications family, and thanks for snagging a copy of this book! Since you've chosen to join us on this journey, we'd like to offer you something special.

Check out the link below for a FREE e-book filled with delightful facts about American History.

But that's not all - you'll also have access to our exclusive email list with even more free e-books and insider knowledge. Well, what are ye waiting for? Click the link below to join and set sail toward exciting adventures in American History.

Access your bonus here
https://ahoypublications.com/
Or, Scan the QR code!

# Table of Contents

# Introduction

The Great Depression started with the U.S. stock market crash on October 29, 1929, known as **Black Tuesday**. Its effects would last for another ten years, affecting the whole world. In the U.S., countless people lost jobs and homes, and farmlands vanished into great Dust Bowls. As children were orphaned and people lived on the streets, the Great Depression also marked a period when ordinary people showed courage and resilience and became resourceful in using whatever they could find. They protested against government unfairness, found hope when there was none, and rose above small differences to stand united against all difficulties.

As we will read some of these amazing stories that sprung up during this time, we will find why these stories can cheer us up even today. While written especially for children, this book is suitable for readers of all ages. The stories will come alive through fascinating images and end-of-chapter activities.

# Chapter One:  The Orphan Train Riders

It was the early 1930s, and the Great Depression struck America. People were without jobs, poverty was widespread, and banks were failing. Factories had begun shutting down, and thousands of children were wandering the streets, homeless, alone, and without parents to care for them. Some had lost their parents to illnesses, while others belonged to families so poor they could no longer afford to care for them.

Charles Loring Brace, a minister and social reformer, was deeply moved by the plight of orphaned children wandering the streets of big cities. Brace thought it would do these children good if they could find a fresh start in some new homes.

Where would that be?

There were orphanages at that time, but a caring and loving home can never compare to an orphanage. Brace firmly believed that children thrived best in a family environment where they could work, learn, and feel loved.

The cities were already overcrowded as well as dangerous for small children without a home. How marvelous it would be to raise these children in rural families that were willing to foster them. It would provide stability, fresh air, and opportunities for work and education in close-knit communities. Brace's idea led to the founding of the Children's Aid Society and the beginning of the Orphan Train Movement.

As we read the real-life story of an orphan child, Arthur Field, we will explore how this idea impacted his and many other lives who were looking for a place to call home.

Young Arthur Field was an orphan who bounced from one foster home to another in New York City. He was five years old and still unadopted. Arthur's plight made him ideal for the orphan train ride. On a fine day, he boarded a train bound for Iowa. Perhaps he would finally have parents and a new home.

### Arthur's Journey

Five-year-old Arthur stood on the crowded platform, clutching his small bundle of belongings. Hundreds of other small children were waiting alongside him. Some looked excited, whispering eagerly, while others seemed nervous, their eyes wide and searching. Suddenly, some children shouted, "Look, there's the train." They all turned toward the tracks.

The train chugged in, its huge engine gleaming under platform lights. To Arthur, the series of connected cars, each with tall windows and dimly lit interiors, looked endless as it rolled into the platform.

Arthur's eyes widened as steam rose around the wheels, hissing. The smell of coal and oil filled the air. They waited patiently for the train to stop, still puffing out steam. Adults hurried the boys through the crowd. Inside, the train cars were lined with hard, wooden benches and narrow aisles. Arthur found a seat by a window next to another small boy. All the boys had grime on their faces, mismatched clothing, and worn shoes.

Arthur looked up and saw a lady holding a basket and smiling down at them. She was Miss Laura Hill from the Children's Aid Society. She would look after the children during the journey with others. The train jerked forward as a loud, sharp whistle filled the air with a smoky soot. Everyone covered their ears then and rubbed the coal dust from their eyes. Soon, the train chugged across open fields dotted with small wooden houses and the occasional red barn. Rivers and trees sped past, and tall grasses swayed as the train hurtled through the countryside.

He craned his neck to see out the window. Cows grazed lazily, farmers worked in the fields, and laundry fluttered on lines – all shrinking – then melting into new scenery.

Arthur watched this for a while. Miss Hill had opened her basket. Arthur could smell freshly baked bread. Suddenly, he was hungry. Miss Hill smiled kindly and said, "Do you want some sandwiches?" Arthur nodded eagerly.

The ladies handed sandwiches and fruit pieces to all the boys. The train soon filled with the sound of munching as the boys eagerly devoured the food.

Iowa was far from New York, and it took several hours for the train to reach. On the way, it stopped at many stations. At each step, local people hopped in and out to travel to their destinations.

Men in dusty overalls tipped their hats at the ladies, and women in sun-faded dresses talked and knitted. Their children gazed at the group of orphans with curiosity. Baskets of farm fresh produce – crisp apples and jars of preserves – hung from the farmer's arms, and they carried jars of fresh milk.

Some orphans were just two years old, and they needed milk. The local farmers quickly stepped in and offered to sell milk and fruits.

Arthur thought about how kind the village women were; they all looked so happy. He wished he could find a place in their hearts. New York, with its bustling streets and honking cars, seemed so far away.

### Arrived At Last

When the train arrived in a small Iowa farming town called Clarinda, Arthur was surprised to see a large group of farmers waiting to greet them at the station.

Arthur wished with all his heart that he could stay here. How nice if this was to be his home. Could that man be his daddy? He was leaning against a wall, puffing on his pipe, and his wife was nearby.

Arthur didn't know why he felt they were his mom and dad and that they had come to take him home. He would not have to go back to the orphanage again. Like all those farmer's children, he could now go to school and play with other kids. When he came home, Mom would have a warm dinner ready. She would read her a storybook in bed while Dad could tuck him safely in for the cold night. Arthur didn't need to fear the cold anymore.

He walked to Worley and Lillian Smith, who had come because they were curious about the train. He climbed onto Worley's lap. Worley hugged him tight. Lillian smiled.

Arthur tilted his face to look at Worley's warm, gentle eyes. He asked softly, "Are you going to be my daddy?"

Lillian's eyes filled with tears.

"Yes, we are your Mom and Dad," she whispered to the boy and kissed him on his forehead.

Arthur found a home that day. Worley and Lillian were the best parents to a child who felt alone and lost in a big, brutal city.

Arthur made a journey that 200,000 children would also take over the span of 75 years in search of a loving home and a better future. They had fear in their hearts: Would they be loved? Would someone want them? They didn't know how the journey would end for them, yet they showed courage by traveling all the way.

Not everyone found a loving home, but those who did had their lives changed for the better. It all started with the dream of a missionary who wanted the orphans to have the care, stability, and sense of belonging that they were missing in New York.

Charles Loring Brace.[1]

Picture of children boarding the orphan train.'

# Activity: Quiz

1. What was the purpose of the Orphan Train?

   a. The train took orphan children from crowded city orphanages to foster homes in rural America.

   b. The train carried the orphans to orphanages.

2. How many children traveled on the Orphan Train over several years?

   a. 100,000

   b. 200,000

3. Who was the founder of the Orphan Train movement?

   a. Charles Lamb.

   b. Charles Loraine Brace.

4. What was the condition of the city orphanages in those days?

   a. Poor.

   b. Excellent.

5. What happened to Arthur Field?

   a. Arthur found a new home in rural America.

   b.Arthur was returned to the New York orphanage.

# Answers

1. a. The train took the children from city orphanages to foster homes in rural America.
2. b. Over the years, 200,000 children traveled by the orphan train.
3. b. Charles Loraine Brace founded the Orphan Train movement.
4. a. The condition of city orphanages was poor during the Great Depression.
5. a. Arthur found a new home in rural America.

# Your Diary Entry

Can you imagine you are on a journey to distant lands alone without your parents? You may close your eyes and think of a small orphan child standing alone, fearful of leaving the city behind for a faraway land they have never seen. Still, there could be a new home there, warm foods, and loving parents.

You may open your eyes and write your story as if you are waiting on the platform and are about to ride the Orphan Train.

# Chapter Two:  The Dust Bowl Miracle

In the 1930s, a terrible disaster called the Dust Bowl struck the American Midwest. Years had gone by without a drop of rain, and the country was already suffering through the Great Depression. Crop prices were so low that farmers didn't earn much money. On top of that, the cost of farming machinery rose steeply.

Farmers tried to make up for this loss by tilling more land, even those unsuitable for farming. They completely abandoned good farming practices, and Mother Nature wasn't happy about any of it.

When the farmers removed vast stretches of sturdy prairie grass, the soil became loose. Where there were once deep-rooted grasses that held the soil together, now dry soil with cracks as thick as a strong worker's hands crisscrossed the land. When strong gusts of wind blew ferociously through fields, the gusty winds blew away the soil, swirling in massive clouds, covering the whole sky like a blanket.

From 1930 to 1940, drought and severe dust storms ravaged farming communities across the Great Plains, especially in Oklahoma, Texas, Kansas, Colorado, and New Mexico, devastating land and families.

### The Dawsons

The Dawsons lived on a modest wheat farm in Oklahoma. Hard work and simple joys filled their days. Mr. Dawson rose before dawn, plowing and planting, while Mrs. Dawson tended to the animals and vegetable garden. Life was not easy, but it was rewarding. Rows of golden wheat swayed under wide blue skies, cows grazed peacefully in green pastures, and the sound of children's laughter rang in the air as they chased chickens. On Sundays, everyone dressed in their best clothes and headed for the church. Neighborhood potluck suppers under the huge oak tree were events to celebrate, sharing food and laughter. Adults talked about their joys and worries while the children played. Life in the village was simple and comforting for everyone.

Then, the rains stopped. The crops in the fields shriveled under the scorching sun. Fierce winds swept through the fields, lifting the loose, dry soil and hurling it at the villages. Dust coated everything – roads, houses, farms, and people – making it difficult to see, breathe, or work. The soil was now light as ash, and towering black clouds blocked the sun. Every corner, floor, and piece of furniture was covered with dust. Families watched in horror as their farmlands turned to barren wastelands.

The Dawsons also watched their harvests vanish. Out of desperation, they decided to leave everything they had and find a home elsewhere. With a heavy heart, they packed their few belongings and stepped out for the unknown future. The home they'd lived in and loved for years was no longer safe.

Would they join the long line of families leaving? They didn't want to. But there was no other choice. Children cried because their breath tasted of grit, burning their throats. Mrs. Dawson was crying, too. Their land had been passed down through generations, and she'd hoped to pass it on to their own children. "My heart is breaking," she sobbed. Mr. Dawson was not happy, either.

He decided to stay and try to find out some methods to rescue their lands. In a heroic act, some other villagers also agreed.

He said, "As a last try, I will dig trenches tomorrow and see what I can do."

### Turning Around

The following day, Mr. Dawson dug trenches and laid sod barriers around the fields. These are grass barriers that can check soil loss and erosion. Mrs. Dawson realized water was the most precious commodity. She used it sparingly to keep a few vegetables alive.

Following their examples, other villagers stepped forward with a strong community spirit. Families shared tools, and men tried contour plowing. This meant they'd till the soil along the land's natural lines, a new skill that could prevent further blow-away. Villagers joined hands to build windbreaks from trees that could shield their fields from the wind. With every small success, rays of hope shone brighter.

The real break came when Mr. Dawson planted sorghum. Wheat is a delicate crop, but sorghum thrives in dry soil; its roots can bind with the soil, even against fierce winds.

"It's working! The soil's holding!" Mr. Dawson grinned, clapping his hands. "We might just beat this dust yet!"

He shared seeds with neighbors, and soon, fields of resilient sorghum dotted the landscape. Mrs. Dawson and other women in the village had already built a community water collection system. They used barrels to catch and save every drop of rainwater. The villagers felt hope as the sorghum stood firm against the wind. Under its shade, they could cultivate other crops.

The survival stories of the Dust Bowl are a legacy of resilience and resourcefulness. They show us that fortune can turn in our favor when we face problems boldly and do hard work. It's important to think about what might help us in any situation rather than simply giving up. When we do this, we're more likely to come up with fresh ideas. This is adaptability.

Community support was also important as they worked through their challenges and learned from their mistakes.

The farmers learned to respect the land and protect the soil, known as sustainable farming, in order to avoid repeating the terrifying Dust Bowl. As stories like these were passed down through generations, their children also learned a deep respect for nature and the strength to face hard times.

A Farm engulfed in the Dust Bowl.[3]

Windbreaks.[4]

Historical Dust Bowl Photo.[5]

# Activities: Quiz

1. The Dust Bowl took place during the 1930s, a time when the Great Depression was already causing hardship.

   a. True

   b. False

2. Removing prairie grass without proper planning made the soil loose and made it easier for the wind to blow it away.

   a. True

   b. False

3. The Dawsons had an easy and carefree life, even during the Dust Bowl.

   a. True

   b. False

4. The Dust Bowl showed that sustainable farming practices were important for protecting the soil and the land.

   a. True

   b. False

5. The Dust Bowl left a lasting lesson for future generations about respecting nature and being adaptable during hard times.

   a. True

   b. False

# Answers

1. a. True
2. a. True
3. b. False
4. a. True
5. a. True

# Dust Bowl Survival Challenge

Hello, young historian! Imagine you've traveled back in time to the 1930s, when giant dust storms turned day into night, and farming families had to be super clever to survive. Your mission, which is going to be quite the challenge, is to help your family make it through the Dust Bowl!

**The scene:** The year is 1935. Your family lives on a farm in Oklahoma. The sky often turns dark with dust, and growing food has become really tough. But you're not giving up! You need to help your family plan how to survive.

## Your Survival Challenge

### Part 1: Protect Your Home

Think about these questions and write down your ideas:

- How will you keep the dust out of your house?
    - HINT: What could you use to seal windows and doors?
    - BONUS: Where or when have you seen people use something to shield the windows?

### Part 2: Food and Water Planning

Go ahead and prepare a list of the following:

- Five foods that can last a long time without going bad
- Three ways to collect and store clean water
- Two ways to protect your vegetable garden from dust

### Part 3: Create A Dust Storm Kit

What would you pack in a special box for when dust storms hit? Make sure you include:

- Things to help you breathe
- Ways to see in the dark
- Items to keep you busy when stuck inside

### Fun Activity: Design Your Dust Mask!

Now, let's try something new! Draw a picture of a dust mask you could make from things found around your house. What materials would you use?

### Family Discussion Questions

Talk about these with your family:

1. What would be the hardest thing about living through the Dust Bowl?

2. What skills do you have that would help your family survive?

3. How is the Dust Bowl similar to the challenges we face today?

### Bonus Challenge: Weather Watcher

Create a weather diary for one week. Compare your weather to what people experienced during the Dust Bowl. How is it different? How is it the same?

Remember: The families who managed to survive the Dust Bowl were creative, brave, and worked together. And that's just what you're doing with this planning activity! They turned their homes into fortresses against the dust and found clever ways to save food and water.

What survival ideas can YOU come up with? Write them down and share them with your family!

*Teacher/Parent Note: This activity encourages critical thinking, historical empathy, and family preparedness discussions while remaining age-appropriate. It can be expanded into a larger unit on Great Depression/Dust Bowl history or environmental science.*

# Chapter Three: The Penny Auction

The Great Depression was a time when America experienced a major economic crisis. This crisis had terrible effects on everyone, especially the farmers.

Farmers took loans from banks to meet the cost of farming. The banks had one condition. They would hold the farmers' lands or houses against the loan. This was called collateral. Farmers had to repay the loan in small monthly amounts. If they failed to make their payments, banks would take away their lands or houses. Although it was scary for farmers to possibly lose their land or homes, they took loans because they needed them.

With the loans, they bought land, seeds, and equipment and paid for repairs on their farms. They planted more crops for a larger harvest. More money meant they could pay back their mortgages. However, when crop prices fell during the Great Depression, they couldn't sell their crops for enough money to repay their loans.

### Auctioning the Farmer's Lands

When many families couldn't repay their loans, banks started taking farms away. Families were heartbroken as they lost everything and could do nothing about it.

Banks held auctions to sell the land, tools, and houses. In an auction, people came from all over to buy them at far lower prices than their actual worth. A person from the bank or the local sheriff was the auctioneer who conducted the auction.

The auctioneer stood where everyone could see him. He then called out each item, such as a tractor, and asked for bids.

"Who will give me three dollars for this tractor?"

Someone from the crowd said, "I'll pay four dollars!"

The auctioneer invited others to bid over this price. The person who offered the highest bid for an item got it, and the money went to the bank.

Farmers watched sadly. It wasn't easy for them because they had worked hard. They lost their livelihood, their memories, and their dreams. Word spread that banks auctioned the land because farmers couldn't pay back a bank loan.

**Penny Auction**

Farmers in a small community were like one big family. They knew each other, met at church gatherings and celebrations, helped each other with farm chores, and stayed together in hard times.

A small community of farmers in a local village in the Midwest devised a clever plan when they learned the land of the Heller family would be sold at auction the next day.

"Only we will bid. And we will bid just a few cents on each item," their chief said.

"What will we do if outsiders bid more?" Heller's neighbor asked.

"We won't allow them to bid. Only people we trust will be in this auction," the chief said firmly.

They quietly spread the word so that only a handful of people learned about their plan.

On auction day, farmers arrived one by one and stood with the crowd. The bidding started. One of the farmers began the bid by a penny. Others remained silent. When an outsider raised his eyebrow and tried to bid, the farmers didn't allow him to speak.

"This is our auction," they said.

Bank officials could do little.

A shiny tractor, the barn, and then the land went for just a few pennies! Heller could buy back everything he owed.

## Community Togetherness

The farmers had big smiles on their faces. They protected their community. Their plan, the Penny Auction, became famous for many reasons.

The farmers carefully planned penny auctions. Neighbors met secretly to choose the buyers they trusted. They arrived early on auction day and stopped others from bidding. Farmers got back their land by bidding just a few pennies.

The farmers knew that if they were caught, the banks could issue a complaint against them, and they could go to prison, but they were not afraid. They wanted to help each other keep their land and livelihoods. As the community stood in unity, the banks had to return the land and houses to the farmers. The story of the penny auction showed how strong communities could stand firm and thrive during the toughest times.

Farmer's Auction.'

Farmers' meet.[7]

Happy Reunion.[8]

# Activity: Quiz

1. During the Great Depression, the banks auctioned farmlands if farmers couldn't repay their loans.
   a. Truth
   b. Lie

2. The farmers paid off their mortgages to the banks for a few pennies.
   a. Truth
   b. Lie

3. The story of Penny Auction is about weak communities.
   a. Truth
   b. Lie

# Answers

1. a. True
2. a. True
3. b. False

# Write a short story on a Penny Auction.

Imagine you are in a town in the Midwest, and an auction will start tomorrow. One of your neighbors will lose his land and house. What will you do as the town leader? Who will you call, and who must not know about your plan? Give them names. Imagine the auctioneer and the outsiders who might come. Make a plan to help your neighbor get their land back tomorrow.

_____

_____

_____

_____

_____

_____

_____

_____

_____

_____

_____

_____

_____

# Chapter Four: The Empire State Building's Construction

America was in the grip of the terrible Great Depression. Many families struggled, businesses closed, and people lost their jobs and homes. People saw no hope. They did not know when or how things would look up again. Something must happen to instill hope and courage in everyone. But what might it be?

### A Symbol

A symbol that would reach the skies might show that America could still achieve amazing things in the midst of adversity. What about building a towering skyscraper that would be taller than any other building in the world?

Why build a towering skyscraper during such hard times? America was struggling, but creating something glorious during such tough times would show that the American people were not afraid of the challenge.

John J. Raskob, a businessman, and Al Smith, a former governor of New York, thought just that when they wanted the Empire State Building to be the tallest structure in the world.

Where would the money come from? Raskob and Smith were determined. Raskob gave money, and other wealthy traders came forward. They had a dream they wanted to share with everyone. Everyone would fight the difficult times together to make a difference. Tough times would come and go, but courageous people would last, just like the Empire State Building.

Thousands of people worked on the project. Many were immigrants and skilled tradespeople who worked through rain, wind, and snow. The work went quickly. Everyone worked together like a giant puzzle team, connecting over 60,000 tons of steel. Masons laid bricks and concrete, while laborers carried heavy materials using ropes, cranes, and carts. Workers climbed high, balancing on beams. Hundreds of people would gather on the streets, watching the building get taller every day, rising toward the sky.

Construction was completed in just over a year – even the builders did not expect it to happen so fast. In May 1931, people in New York City craned their necks to look at the majestic skyscraper, which stood over 100 stories tall!

The Empire State Building was the tallest in the world at the time. People called it a "miracle of the Great Depression." It stood for hope and strength, a structure only the legendary ape King Kong could expect to climb.

Americans felt pride and confidence. New Yorkers thought it was more than just a building. The Empire State Building was a monument to the courageous and determined people who believed that America could rise above any challenge with hard work, resilience, and hope.

Today, people come from all over the world to see the magnificent Empire State Building in New York City. It reminds us that people can overcome adversity and climb great heights despite their problems when they put their minds to it.

Empire State Building Under Construction.'

Empire State Building.[10]

# Activity: Quiz

1. The Empire State Building was the tallest building in the world when it was built.

    a. True

    b. False

2. It took many years to build the Empire State Building.

    a. True

    b. False

3. The Empire State Building was built in Chicago.

    a. True

    b. False

# Answers

1. a. True
2. a. True
3. b. False

# Image Research Task

Can you find images of the Empire State Building when it was built? Can you place them in order if you find several of them? You can paste them into a scrapbook if your pictures are in print. Don't forget to mention the dates of the images.

# Chapter Five: The School That Grew From The Dust

No one wants to feel hardships, pain, or challenges. However, we become our best when facing them with courage and determination. The Great Depression was no different. There are innumerable tales of ordinary Americans showing great courage, hope, and unity to improve their lives. One such tale is about how an organization came forward when, one after another, schools closed down.

During the Great Depression, many people were without jobs, and communities could not support basic needs, including public buildings. Schools were falling apart in many communities because there was no money to repair them. With broken windows, leaky ceilings, and crumbling walls, they were unsafe for children. Families and teachers were worried about their kids' education without a place for learning.

### Building Schools

The Civil Works Administration (CWA) was a government program that created new jobs and provided services to help people. One such activity was funding schools. When they decided to set up new schools, teachers, parents, and workers joined in to help the movement.

The task was not easy. Very little money was available, so communities often ran out of supplies such as bricks and wood. Many materials were old or scarce. Working outdoors was difficult in winter due to snow and icy winds. They did not have heating the way we do today.

Still, the townspeople pressed on, determined to create a safe learning place for kids. When materials were unavailable, resourceful workers reused scraps and fixed them with worn-out tools. Skilled tradespeople laid bricks, carpenters repaired desks, and teachers volunteered to prepare classrooms.

Teachers in CWA-supported schools worked for lower wages. They did not mind creating lessons and teaching in rickety classrooms or even using chalkboards made from painted plywood. Some teachers volunteered to teach double shifts.

**CWA School**

Pine Ridge, South Dakota, was a rural town. During the Great Depression, children had no classrooms and learned only bits of reading and math. Then, the CWA built a new school that changed everything. Such schools came up in Texas, Michigan, and many other places.

Teachers taught students the real power of education. They wanted their students to dream of becoming doctors, writers, and teachers.

The teachers were locals and volunteers who traveled from other places. Students learned traditional skills alongside books. Teachers often collected books from nearby towns to teach their students; some teachers taught students after school years.

CWA schools gave countless children an opportunity to learn, dream, and break free from poverty. Communities became stronger, and with education, children had more opportunities nationwide.

Children attending a CWA-built school.[11]

Workers Constructing a School.[12]

Basic Classroom.[18]

# Activities: Quiz

1. What happened to the schools during the Great Depression?

    a. Schools closed down due to a lack of funds.

    b. The Great Depression had no impact on schools.

2. Why were the parents worried?

    a. The children played all day.

    b. Children couldn't go to school.

3. What did the CWA build?

    a. Warships

    b. Schools

4. Did the teachers work voluntarily for CWA schools?

    a. Teachers got good salaries.

    b. Most worked voluntarily.

5. Which organization helped the children to study and learn?

    a. CWA

    b. CAW

# Answers

1. a. Schools closed down during the Great Depression due to a lack of funds.
2. b. The parents were worried because their children couldn't go to school.
3. b. The CWA helped build schools.
4. b. Most teachers worked voluntarily.
5. b. The Civil Works Administration helped the children to study and learn.

# Draw Your School As The CWA Builds It

Imagine you're watching the CWA workers build a new school for you from the beginning. Can you draw in step-by-step as the school gradually comes up?

# Chapter Six: Hobos And Their Secret Signs

Many stories of strong and resourceful people come to light during the Great Depression. This will be a story about signs.

You may have seen your parents stop their car just before a line at an intersection, even when no cars were crossing the street. This is because there was probably a stop sign. That sign tells the car's driver to come to a full stop and make sure there is no traffic coming from the cross street. Signs are everywhere and include directions for parking, cycling, or not to trespass. Everyone learns about these road signs to keep the roads safe. You even have to take a test showing that you know what the signs mean before you are even given a driver's permit.

What if there is another type of road sign – so faint that it is easy to miss? These mysterious signs tell more stories than merely stop, do not enter, or go. During the Great Depression, a group of people known as *hobos* used signs to keep each other safe. The story of the Hobos is strange and often misunderstood.

## The Hobos

Railway building began in 1866. As the country struggled after the Civil War, workers willingly traveled across the country to build new tracks. Farmers and laborers hopped onto slow freight trains to travel for work during harvest seasons, in mines, or timber camps. It's unclear why they earned the nickname *hobos*.

Unlike tramps or bums, who rarely worked, the hobos wanted to work. However, the difficulty in finding work required them to travel great distances, primarily by train. This led to a unique lifestyle known as the hobo life. During the Great Depression, thousands of people found themselves jobless, taking on the hobo life.

People believed hobos only traveled by train. However, they also traveled by car and on foot. Traveling is exciting, but it can also be risky and hard. Riding on a train without a ticket is illegal and can get you in a lot of trouble. Besides, jumping on a moving train is dangerous. The jumper may slide and sustain injuries or even death.

Once on the train, hobos tried to avoid punishment by hiding themselves inside or among the freight goods. Sometimes, they failed to emerge from their hideouts, resulting in tragic deaths. Still, "rail riding" was a hobo way of life.

The locals were not friendly to them. They believed that hobos were homeless and lazy, confusing them with tramps or bums. Who would want to trust such individuals? The cops chased them off trains and made them leave their camps, which were makeshift shelters. Women hobos faced the same dangers as men, such as starvation and harsh weather, but they were also more likely to be hurt by people while traveling. Despite the danger, many women fearlessly joined the hobo community and showed courage against hardship.

### The Hobo Signs

Hobos had to protect themselves. To do that, they came up with a secret system of signs to help each other. Despite their constant travels, their paths frequently crossed. They drew symbols on fences, buildings, and trees. All the signs shared useful tips. "A kind lady lives here," was a smiling face, while a circle with two arrows was a warning to get out fast! Signs told hobos where to find food, safe places to sleep, or places to avoid danger. In this manner, they established a robust community that cared for each other – despite their lack of familiarity. It was their way of staying safe and connected while traveling to unknown places during difficult times.

### The Story of a Hobo

Doyle E. Marion was sixteen years old when he rode the Union Pacific Railroad's massive locomotives up into the Siskiyou Mountains. The train came to a stop around daylight one morning when he got off with others. They headed down to a rainforest, where they met a hobo community. Marion recalled sharing hot coffee with the group. To Marion, who was covered in soot and exhausted, the hot cup of coffee in the cold morning air tasted the finest he ever had. Marion's Union Pacific Railroad trip memories and others are about railroading history and hobo culture. He met hobos in remote mountains and jungles while traveling for jobs. Their warm welcome touched Marion. His later life is unknown, although such stories describe strangers' kindness during the most difficult times.

### Lasting Effect on American Culture

Hobos liked to travel alone. However, they met in hobo jungles. These were makeshift camps often located near railroads, as hobos commonly traveled by hopping freight trains. Hobo jungles provided a place for rest and cooking meals over small fires.

Sometimes, they traveled with a companion until one decided to take a new route. Despite their solitary life, the hobos had a strong obligation to help their community people, which led to the invention of the signs and symbols. The way they traveled on moving trains was dangerous; one wrong step could result in serious injury or death. They also had to avoid railroad security agents, known as "bulls," who either chased them off the trains or mistreated them. Few people could offer work or food during the Great Depression; hobos faced hunger and a lack of shelter. They faced harsh weather conditions, suffered from malnutrition, and had limited access to medical care. Still, they chose to live freely and with a strong will to survive all the obstacles.

A hobo and writings on a fence indicating the nearest water source.[14]

Secret Hobo Signs.[15]

Hobos sharing information.[16]

# Activities

## Fill in the Blanks

1. People who traveled for work or food during the Great Depression were called _____.

2. The _____traveled but did not work.

3. The _____ chased the hobos off the trains.

4. The hobos created _____to communicate.

5. The hobos were _____ and _____.

# Answers

1. Hobos
2. Tramps
3. Bulls
4. Signs
5. Resilient and resourceful

# Create Secret Signs

Can you create your own set of secret signs to communicate with your friends?

# Chapter Seven: Soup Kitchen Saviors

The Great Depression was a difficult time for everyone. People lost jobs and homes – and went hungry for days on end. However, this was also when thousands of volunteers came forward with brilliant ideas to help others. These exceptional ideas showed human qualities such as resilience, generosity, and compassion, which brought communities together to fight adversity. One such idea was setting up soup kitchens that provided food to millions in dire need.

### The Widespread Hunger and Poverty

During the Great Depression, factories shut down, jobs vanished, and parents struggled to put food on the table because there were few jobs. Without a job, there was no way to pay for food, no matter how affordable it was. The grocery shelves were stacked with food. Still, children went to bed hungry, their bellies growling empty. Farmers could not sell their products to earn money since agricultural prices had fallen so low that selling their produce barely met the costs. They watched helplessly as food went to waste even while people went hungry. Hunger was everywhere. Something had to be done.

### Soup Kitchens

Soup kitchens became a lifesaver for many families. The idea of soup kitchens that offered free meals to people who couldn't afford food existed before the Great Depression. However, they became more widespread during this period. It was essential to provide starving families with at least some food. They remembered better times and exchanged tips for staying warm and finding work, food, and shelter. Community participation and sharing individual stories gave comfort.

### A Place to Share And Care

During this time, many people came together in order to help prepare community meals and feed thousands of people, even some you wouldn't expect. Al Capone was a Chicago gangster. He was unpopular for his criminal activities. Everyone criticized how he became so wealthy. Capone wanted to appear as a generous and caring figure, and opening soup kitchens that would feed many was just the idea he needed to gain people's sympathy.

Al Capone opened the first soup kitchen in Chicago in 1930. Thousands of hungry people came to his kitchen for hot meals like soup and bread.

You may have heard about the fabled character Robinhood, who stole from the rich to give to the poor. He did it out of a sense of justice. But Capone wanted popularity and fame. It was an act of kindness, nevertheless, and it gave him goodwill. The idea soon spread across the country. Churches, charities, and communities came forward to help those in need.

Volunteers opened soup kitchens all across the country. Long lines of hungry people, including parents and children, stretched down streets, waiting for their turn to eat simple meals like soup, bread, and sometimes coffee. People volunteered to prepare and distribute food. In a gigantic community kitchen, strangers sat together, sharing stories. Such acts made them feel united. They felt strong and comforted. These kitchens became more than a place to eat – they were places that offered warmth of heart.

### Inside The Kitchen

Although churches and private charity organizations were the initial ones to organize soup kitchens, eventually, the state and federal governments stepped in during the mid-1930s. Every city and town had a soup kitchen. People went to the place that was nearest to them. In New York City, for example, the Salvation Army operated kitchens that served hundreds daily. Soup was the main item served. It was easy and inexpensive to make additional soup by adding water. The kitchens relied on donations of food, money, and time from the community.

Every day, a flurry of activity began early in the morning within the kitchens. Volunteers cooked simple meals in large pots. People started lining up well before the food was ready, eager to avoid the rush. There were times when they had to wait hours for a meal. Volunteers served enough food but did not waste resources. Despite limited supplies, these lifelines fed thousands of starving people while fostering hope and resilience during one of America's hardest times.

Volunteers worked tirelessly in soup kitchens, often giving their money in addition to their time to help others. In Chicago and other cities, church groups like the Salvation Army ran kitchens. The volunteers cooked, cleaned, and served meals to hundreds daily. Capuchin Services Center in southeast Detroit served almost 1,500 to 3,000 people daily.

Many of the volunteers were also poor, but they believed in kindness and community service. Their efforts reflected compassion, a noble feeling when people care for everyone. Soup kitchens symbolized unity. Communities came together to help those in need, even though money was scarce for everyone. Soup kitchen volunteers had to start early. Work began with peeling and chopping veggies, stirring big pots of soup, cutting loaves, and setting tables. Their hands moved tirelessly, as they knew soon the kitchen would be open and people would pour over with their plates. They served meals with a smile and cleaned up afterward.

### The Legacy

The soup kitchen legacy continues even today, as modern charities and food banks provide meals and hope for many families unable to pay for food. But they are not just a way to show generosity and care for others. Workers and organizers find deep satisfaction through their selfless service to others. While feeding others and making them happy, the volunteers also felt joy in their hearts.

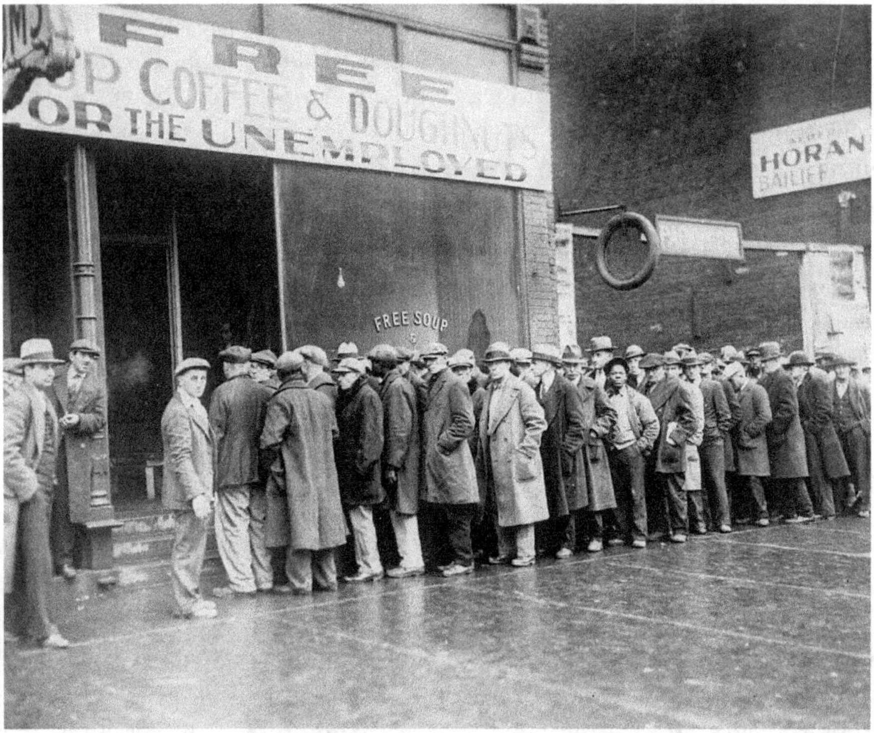


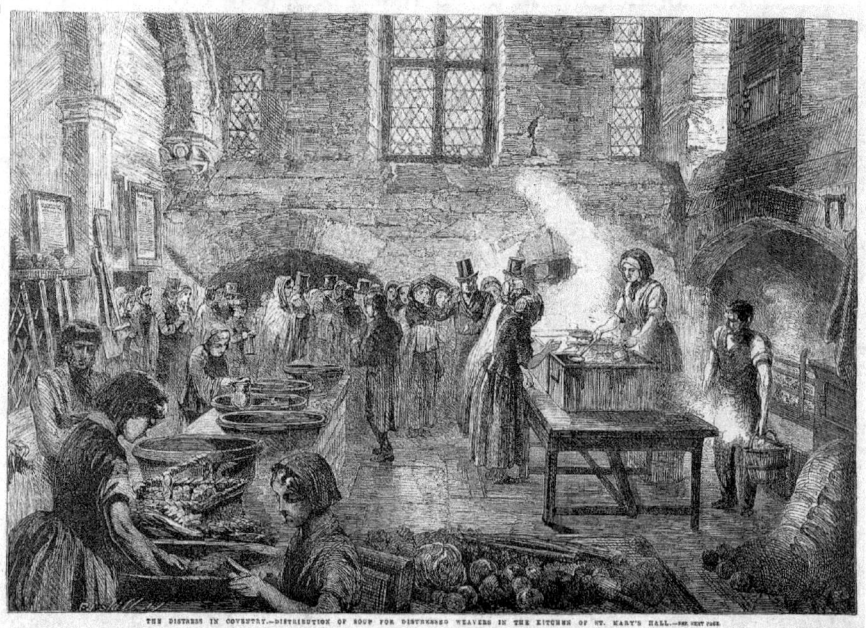

A Long line of people outside a soup kitchen.[17]

THE DISTRESS IN COVENTRY.—DISTRIBUTION OF SOUP FOR DISTRESSED WEAVERS IN THE KITCHEN OF ST. MARY'S HALL.—SEE NEXT PAGE.

Volunteers Preparing Soup.[18]

A Diverse Group Of People Partaking Meals.[19]

# Activities:

## Quiz

1. The first soup kitchen was opened in New York.
    a. True
    b. False
2. Al Capone volunteered in the soup kitchen.
    a. True
    b. False
3. Soup kitchens were owned by state governments.
    a. True
    b. False

# Answers

1. b. False
2. a. True
3. b. False

# Fun-Filled Volunteering

Can you think of different ways you can help your community? You can participate in a food bank, helping others to sort packed food boxes or donations. You can help your neighbor with yard work, carry their groceries, or walk their dog. You may keep your environment clean by picking up litter in your neighborhood. Consider another enjoyable activity, such as volunteering at an animal shelter. Your small acts can make a big difference!

# Chapter Eight:  The Bonus Army
# March On Washington

The government promised bonuses to World War I (1914-1918) veterans for their wartime service but failed to keep it. The veterans learned they would receive it only in 1945. Meanwhile, the country experienced the Great Depression in 1930. The severe financial crunch affected everyone, but the retired war veterans had no income or bonus. Thousands of veterans marched to Washington, D.C., in 1932 to bring attention to the situation. Their army was called the Bonus Army. The veterans stayed in makeshift camps and went through severe hardship while protesting. The government refused to relent and sent soldiers to remove the protesters. Their camps were destroyed. The veterans left, but their stories spread far and wide as a tale of bravery and perseverance against injustice.

### The Bonus Army

World War I ended in 1918. The U.S. Army could not employ all returning World War I veterans due to the reduced need for soldiers during peacetime. Discharged veterans returned to civilian life. The government encouraged them to find civilian work. However, during the Great Depression, many veterans were unemployed, homeless, or facing poverty. They needed money to survive.

The government promised them bonuses as a thank-you for their military service. However, this was intended to be a retirement benefit and would not be available until 1945. Because of their desperate circumstances during the depression, veterans demanded early release of their bonus. Unfortunately, people weren't the only ones suffering financially during this time; the government, struggling with a collapsing economy, claimed it could not pay the bonuses early. If they did, it would worsen the economic crisis. The veterans were frustrated. They felt the nation had abandoned them when they were in need.

### The Protest March

A group of World War I veterans who demanded early payment of their service bonuses started a movement under a former Army sergeant, Walter W. Waters. Waters organized a protest march to Washington, D.C., and submitted a petition to Congress. Word spread quickly as thousands came from all over the country to join the march. Many couldn't afford train tickets, so they hopped on freight trains or walked long distances. The press called it a "Bonus Army." As an "army," the veterans showed unity in their common goal of demanding their promised bonuses. What did the veterans call their force? Their official name was the Bonus Expeditionary Force (BEF), named after their wartime service as the American Expeditionary Forces.

In the summer of 1932, approximately 20,000 veterans and their families arrived in Washington, D.C. Walter W. Waters became the movement's leader. They knew they would have to stay in the city until the Congress discussed their demands. It was difficult to find shelter for thousands of people. The only option was to build a temporary town on the Anacostia Flats with tents and makeshift shelters. Makeshift camps were called "Hoovervilles," and they were made of tents and scraps of wood. Small communities of veterans formed the "Bonus City."

### The Attack

In peaceful gatherings, veterans held marches and speeches, sharing the reasons for their protests. They knew they would have to be calm to avoid police harassment. Despite this, President Hoover ordered the U.S. Army to clear the Bonus City. The army under General Douglas MacArthur attacked the veteran settlement. They used tear gas to dispel the crowd, and their tanks rolled in, demolishing the tents and burning the camps. William Hushka, a survivor of World War I, was in the protest march when the army launched its attack on the veteran settlement. Hushka died during the confrontation.

## The Aftermath

After the violent attack on the peaceful Bonus Army, Americans were outraged. The incident was more tragic because the veterans were protesting with their families. Photographs and newspaper stories depicted the army using tear gas on innocent protestors, burning their shelters, and forcing their families to flee. Most felt the government's actions were unfair and heartless to those who had served the country.

In 1936, due to growing public sympathy, Congress relented and passed a law granting early bonus payments. The story of the brave soldiers remained a beacon of hope for many future protests against unfairness and the importance of standing up for one's rights. It inspired future policies such as the GI Bill, which provided education and housing benefits to veterans after World War II.

Bonus Army in the U.S. Capitol.[20]

Veterans' Makeshift Camps in Washington.[31]

Shacks Burning After Military Attack.[32]

# Activities: Timeline Quiz

Can you arrange the following events in their timeline?

1. The Bonus Army marched to Washington, D.C.
2. End of World War I.
3. The Great Depression started.
4. Congress paid early bonuses to veterans.

# Answer

The correct order of timeline is 2, 3, 1, and 4.

# Make a Diary Entry As a War Veteran

Suppose you time-traveled to America during the Great Depression of 1930. In this world, imagine you are a World War I veteran. You lack the necessary funds to purchase essentials. However, the bonuses that serve as your compensation will allow you to live a better life. Only Congress is preventing the payments from being released. Suddenly, you see hope. Thousands of other veterans give a war cry, "Let's march to Washington D.C."

Can you make successive diary entries as the events unfold from here? Write about your hope and your disappointment. Use feelings, sights, and sounds to make it real!

# Chapter Nine: Hoovervilles: Communities of Hope

Stepping back into the 1930s, a time traveler could see clusters of makeshift homes built from scraps of wood, metal sheets, cloths, and cardboard. These were shantytowns, known as Hoovervilles, strewn across cities and vacant fields. Families who had lost everything to the Great Depression called these homes. The time traveler could see smoke rising from fires lit by people to cook whatever food they could find and keep themselves warm. Hoovervilles were unattractive and filthy. People faced hardship, disease, and a lack of basic facilities. Despite that, the communities showed great strength as they pushed through the challenges.

## The Impact of the Great Depression On People

During the Great Depression, ordinary Americans faced untold miseries. The main problem was job losses as factories closed down and workplaces laid off workers. In rural areas, farmers did not get enough money from selling crops. The cost of farming was sky-high. Millions could not afford rent or mortgages and lost their homes and belongings.

## The Hoovervilles

Finding no other way, families packed their belongings into old cars or wagons and set off searching for work in other places. But where would they stay? They did not have money to pay for rent or housing. Their only choice was to settle in Hoovervilles - makeshift towns on the city's outskirts.

These shantytowns, built out of wood, tin, rags, and cardboard, had no running water or electricity. Sometimes, entire families lived in cars. When people lost their homes and jobs, they also lost their sense of stability and honor. This was what hurt everyone the most. Their only hope came in the form of community friendship and support.

Forced to leave their homes, people constructed temporary shelters in their new settlements. The land did not belong to them, and they had no permission to build proper brick houses or permanent structures. They were forced to use disposable items. These homes could not provide warmth, shelter, or peace and quiet, but residents had no choice.

As more and more people arrived in cities in search of work and food, settlement after settlement sprang up across the country. People named these settlements Hoovervilles after President Herbert Hoover, whom many held responsible for their struggles.

### Life in Hooverville

The people of Hooverville remained resilient in the face of struggles and hardships. They discovered the power of creating communities, not just individual homes. Their old towns and villages had churches, schools, and open places where people gathered after work to relax and talk, and children played. To give Hoovervilles a community, people built makeshift schools and small churches out of the same materials they used to make their shelters. This way, their children could learn, and families could worship.

The settlements had open spaces where neighbors could gather. In one of the largest Hoovervilles in Seattle, the residents organized their community government; Jesse Jackson was their unofficial mayor. Residents held meetings, created rules, and worked together to keep the area clean. Bit by bit, people worked to bring back routine in their lives. Parents taught their kids lessons in handmade classrooms. Some created small markets, and others cooked community meals they shared. Together, they carried out repair work and helped each other with their skills. Families wanted to stay hopeful and maintain a sense of normal life. By working together, they could make the best of their tough situation.

Each Hooverville was different. Small ones had five to ten shanties, while larger ones had thousands. Life was difficult, especially for women, older people, and children. Most homes collapsed during severe rains or storms. There was no protection from the cold. Water was scarce. They had to gather it from nearby ponds or river water. Drinking it was unsafe. For sanitation, they dug ditches to use as latrines – a type of outdoor toilet. Poor living conditions led to illness and disease. When people couldn't afford food or homes, they certainly couldn't afford a doctor. There were volunteers, but there were just too many people living so close to meet all of their needs.

Men searched for work, and women cooked meals, trying to make food last. People used whatever they could find. A few grew vegetable gardens. Kids scavenged "garbage mounds" for materials to fix their homes. People added to or removed junk from these mounds while they worked. Sometimes, someone would bring old car parts for stoves or make pieces of furniture. Children played games with the junk. It was dangerous. Still, some beautiful artworks emerged from their effort.

### The Legacy

The story of Hoovervilles was about community strength and resilience. For those who made Hoovervilles their homes, scraps and throw-away items were useful resources. They got creative in turning junk into useful things. People learned the power of community, which gave them unity and strength. In many ways, Hoovervilles reminds us of the struggles faced during the Great Depression and the role of community in overcoming hardships.

Hooverville.²⁸

Daily Life in Hooverville.[24]

A Makeshift School.[25]

# Activities:

## Quiz

1. When were the Hoovervilles built?
   - a. During the Great Depression
   - b. After the Great Depression
2. Who built the Hoovervilles?
   - a. Government
   - b. Homeless people
3. What kind of settlement was Hooverville?
   - a. Temporary
   - b. Permanent
4. Why were they called Hoovervilles?
   - a. After President Howard Hoover
   - b. They could be disposed of easily.
5. What were the living conditions of people in Hoovervilles?
   - a. Joyful
   - b. Unhealthy

# Answers

1. a. During the Great Depression
2. b. Homeless people
3. a. Temporary
4. a. After President Howard Hoover
5. b. Unhealthy

# Drawing Activity

Imagine you are making your own home in Hooverville during the Great Depression. What would you want it to look like? Will it be a tent? Or do you want to make a yurt? A hut could be another option. Draw your Hooverville house using materials such as tin sheets, scraps of wood, cardboard, or cloth. Would it have a stove made from old car parts? You can also have a tiny garden. Show how you can make a cozy home despite tough times!

# Chapter Ten: Woody Guthrie: The Boy Who Sang For Change

Long ago, storytellers called bards traveled from town to town. They sang and told stories to inspire and bring hope. In the dusty towns of Oklahoma during the Great Depression, a bard roamed the streets with his guitar, meeting farmers, workers, and families who had lost everything. His name was Woody Guthrie, and he would listen keenly to the struggles of ordinary people and turn their stories into songs. Woody's music became a powerful voice for those who had none, inspiring change and bringing hope to many throughout difficult times.

## Early Life

Woodie Guthrie's family lived in a small agricultural and railroad town in Oklahoma. The town became prosperous when oil was discovered. Guthrie was born in 1912. His mother introduced him to the world of music. But times changed, and the once prosperous town lost its glory. Guthrie's mother was ill, and his father had to move away to find work. Guthrie went to live with his other family members in Texas in 1929, where he learned guitar from Jeff Guthrie, a talented fiddler who had won regional contests. Woody married Mary Jennings in 1933.

Guthrie loved the call of the road as much as he loved music. The plight of the people he met during the Great Depression deeply affected Guthrie. When drought turned acres of agricultural land into the Dust Bowl, Guthrie took to the road. He mingled with other displaced people and headed for the West.

**A Voice to The Hopeless**

Guthrie took up odd jobs as he traveled. He played his guitar and harmonica and sang in taverns. A wanderer and an explorer, Guthrie visited hobo camps, traveled by freight train, hitchhiked, and sometimes walked miles. He sang people's songs that lifted everyone's hearts. He wanted his songs to give hope to people who were feeling like they would lose everything. So he sang,

*All around me, a voice was sounding*

*This land was made for you and me.*

The times were hard, and life was difficult for everyone. But like everything, difficulties would also fade away. His songs made everyone wipe their tears and work with energy and pride, believing in themselves.

Everyone was going through difficulties. As the depression dragged on, people gave up hope. Without hope, people became sad. Guthrie wanted them to find strength to face challenges, find solutions, and keep moving forward. He knew only hope could make people think and work hard, build teams, and make changes. But what could he do to make people feel that hope? This was when he found the power of music. He could capture the truth about people and places. He could tell them that they were hard-working people caught up in difficult times. They should not give up on their dreams and stop trying.

Guthrie found that many of the old patriotic songs could not inspire people because they did not reflect the conditions of the Great Depression or the Dust Bowl. People wanted to hear about their stories – stories of sadness, hopes, and dreams. He wrote the song titled *This Land Is Your Land* in 1940. He sang about the beauty of America and reminded people that it was their country. This belief helped people come together, help one another, and work to make things fair for everyone. Everyone had a part to play in improving the country.

Guthrie traveled all over the country with his guitar. He performed in union halls and encouraged workers to unite, demanding fair treatment. He went inside the migrants' camps, talked to the families who struggled to survive, and sang songs that made them feel less alone. Workers on a strike demanding better job payments and work conditions listened to Woody's music to keep fighting. His songs were for everyone. People sang his songs like anthems, which brought people together. They could make a difference when they united.

Woody Guthrie's songs influenced famous musicians like Pete Seeger and Bob Dylan, who inspired people to bring change and fight for justice through music. Guthrie's music lives on, even after the Great Depression. Songs of fairness and hope helped people during the Civil Rights and Workers' Rights movements. Even today, his music can unite, spread hopeful messages, and inspire everyone to believe in the best.

Couple Listening to Radio.[36]

FDR sitting at his desk in the White House, delivering a Fireside Chat.[27]

# Activities:

**Timeline Quiz**

1. When was Guthrie born?

   a. 1930

   b. 1912

2. When did Guthrie go to Texas?

   a. 1932

   b. 1929

3. When did Guthrie marry?

   a. 1930

   b. 1933

4. When did Guthrie realize the power of music to reflect peoples' stories?

   a. 1928

   b. 1930

5. When did Guthrie write *This Land is Your Land?*

   a. 1940

   b. 1938

# Answers

1. b. 1912
2. b. 1929
3. b. 1933
4. b. 1930
5. a. 1940

# Song Lyrics Activity

Listen to Woody Guthrie's "This Land Is Your Land" and write a few lines about the world you want to see.

For example:

*Imagine every child has food to eat,*

*And neighbors smile when they meet.*

*In a world where people live in peace*

*I dream of kindness and sharing that will never cease.*

# End of Book Quiz

1. Which train carried orphans from city orphanages to rural foster homes during the Great Depression?

    a. The Orphan Train

    b. Freight trains

2. Why did the Dust Bowl happen?

    a. Farmers ignored good farming methods.

    b. Due to a lack of rain

3. What was the most successful part of the penny auction story?

    a. The farmers got rid of bank officials.

    b. The farmers bought back their land for a penny.

4. What do you think the Empire State Building signifies?

    a. A symbol of "we can."

    b. The tallest building in the world.

5. Why were the parents proud of CWA schools during the Great Depression?

    a. They taught discipline to children.

    b. They provided education for children for free.

6. Who used special symbols as a way of communication?

    a. Tramps

    b. Hobos

7. How did soup kitchens help people during the Great Depression?
   a. They supplied free meals.
   b. People could be paid to work in these kitchens.

8. Who participated in the Bonus Army March?
   a. Soldiers
   b. Veterans

9. What do you think the word *Hoovervilles* stands for?
   a. Shantytowns
   b. High-rise buildings

10. Who sang for change during the Great Depression?
    a. Woody Guthrie
    b. Bob Dylan

# Answers

1. a. The Orphan Train
2. a. Farmers ignored good farming methods
3. b. The farmers bought back their land for a penny
4. a. A symbol of "we can"
5. b. CWA schools provided education for children for free
6. b. Hobos
7. a. Soup kitchens supplied free meals
8. b. Veterans
9. a. Shantytowns
10. a. Woody Guthrie

# Check out another book in the series

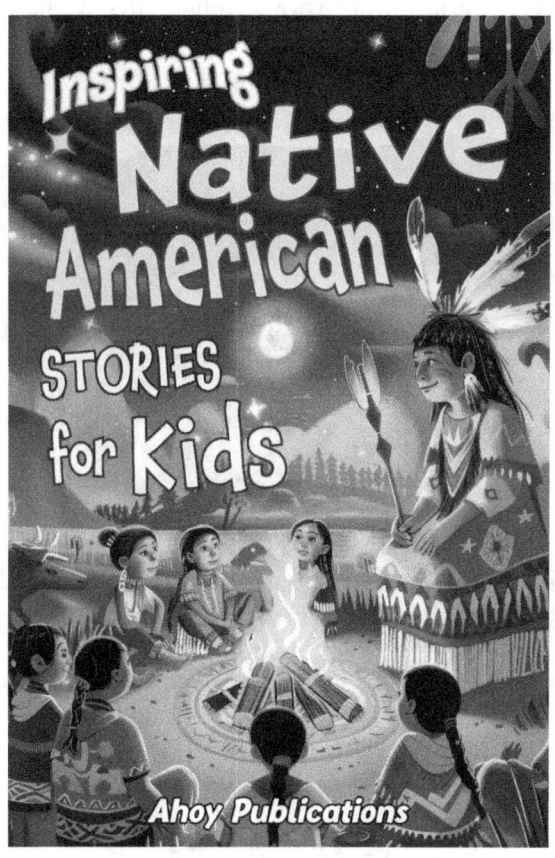

# Welcome Aboard, Check Out This Limited-Time Free Bonus!

Ahoy, reader! Welcome to the Ahoy Publications family, and thanks for snagging a copy of this book! Since you've chosen to join us on this journey, we'd like to offer you something special.

Check out the link below for a FREE e-book filled with delightful facts about American History.

But that's not all - you'll also have access to our exclusive email list with even more free e-books and insider knowledge. Well, what are ye waiting for? Click the link below to join and set sail toward exciting adventures in American History.

Access your bonus here
https://ahoypublications.com/
Or, Scan the QR code!

# References

Brown, A. (2019, January 22). *Orphan Trains.* Social Welfare History Project. https://socialwelfare.library.vcu.edu/programs/child-welfarechild-labor/orphan-trains/

Burlbow, L. (2011). Keeping Schools Open in Depression Era Texas: The CWA and the 1933-34 School Year. *East Texas Historical Journal, 49,* 3-2011. https://core.ac.uk/download/pdf/72738208.pdf

Jackson, M. A. (2015). *Rambling Round: The Life and Times of Woody Guthrie | Articles and Essays | Woody Guthrie and the Archive of American Folk Song: Correspondence, 1940-1950 | Digital Collections | Library of Congress.* The Library of Congress. https://www.loc.gov/collections/woody-guthrie-correspondence-from-1940-to-1950/articles-and-essays/rambling-round-the-life-and-times-of-woody-guthrie/

National Drought Mitigation Center. (2022). *The Dust Bowl.* Drought.unl.edu; National Drought Mitigation Center. https://drought.unl.edu/dustbowl/

National Orphan Train Complex. (2021). *Arthur Field Smith – National Orphan Train Complex.* Orphantraindepot.org. https://orphantraindepot.org/arthur-field-smith/

National Security Agency. (2021, August 4). *Hobo Communications: A Brief History of Hobos and Their Signs.* National Security Agency/Central Security Service. https://www.nsa.gov/History/National-Cryptologic-Museum/Exhibits-Artifacts/Exhibit-View/Article/2718897/hobo-communications-a-brief-history-of-hobos-and-their-signs/

Oak Crest Intermediate School. (2010, January 6). *Soup Kitchens 1930s.* SlideShare. https://www.slideshare.net/slideshow/soup-kitchens-1930s/2842828

PapersOwl. (2024, May 21). *A Glimpse into the Lives of Hoovervilles: America's Shantytowns of the Great Depression - Free Essay Example | PapersOwl.com*. PapersOwl.com. https://papersowl.com/examples/a-glimpse-into-the-lives-of-hoovervilles-americas-shantytowns-of-the-great-depression/

PBS Online. (2019). *BUILDING BIG: Databank: Empire State Building*. Pbs.org. https://www.pbs.org/wgbh/buildingbig/wonder/structure/empire_state.html

Seaver, C. (2022, November 14). *What Was Life Like in the Hoovervilles of the Great Depression?* https://www.historydefined.net/hoovervilles/

Steinsworth, C. (2024). *The History of the Empire State Building in Midtown Manhattan, New York City*. Steinsworth.com. https://steinsworth.com/the-history-of-the-empire-state-building-in-midtown-manhattan-new-york-city/

Uys, E. L. (2021). *Hobo Life in the Great Depression*. Erroluys.com. https://erroluys.com/greatdepressionarchive2.html

Working Class History. (2024). *Penny Auctions*. Workingclasshistory.com. https://stories.workingclasshistory.com/article/10662/penny-auctions

# Image Sources

[1] *https://archive.org/details/lifeofcharleslor00bracuoft/page/n9/mode/2up*

[2] *See page for author, CC BY-SA 4.0 <https://creativecommons.org/licenses/by-sa/4.0>, via Wikimedia Commons https://upload.wikimedia.org/wikipedia/commons/a/a9/Orphan_Train.jpg*

[3] *https://commons.wikimedia.org/wiki/File:Dust_Bowl_farm._Coldwater_District%2C_north_of_Dalhart%2C_Texas.jpg*

[4] *https://commons.wikimedia.org/wiki/File:Shelterbelts-_Windbreaks_-_Kansas_-_DPLA_-_6c3913da93cf2053c7a6e60245351311.jpg*

[5] *https://commons.wikimedia.org/wiki/File:Dust_Bowl_-_Dallas%2C_South_Dakota_1936.jpg*

[6] *https://commons.wikimedia.org/wiki/File:Auctioning_off_a_team_of_horses_at_the_closing-out_sale_of_Frank_Sheroan%2C_tenant_farmer_-_DPLA_-_9e4a563c2751872bae26a3aecd528f0a.jpg*

[7] *https://commons.wikimedia.org/wiki/File:The_farmers_teams_(2447211173).jpg*

[8] *From family photo album of Infrogmation., CC BY-SA 2.0 <https://creativecommons.org/licenses/by-sa/2.0>, via Wikimedia Commons https://commons.wikimedia.org/wiki/File:GGrandHug.jpg*

[9] *Lewis Hine, CC0, via Wikimedia Commons https://commons.wikimedia.org/wiki/File:Icarus%2C_Empire_State_Building_MET_DT1655.jpg*

[10] *Mark Asthoff qa9de, CC0, via Wikimedia Commons https://commons.wikimedia.org/wiki/File:Empire_State_Building_%28cropped%29.jpg*

[11] *https://commons.wikimedia.org/wiki/File:CWA%2C_Recreation_%26_Leisure_Time%2C_%22Orchestral_training_for_grade_and_high_school_students.%22_-_NARA_-_196015.tif*

[12] *https://commons.wikimedia.org/wiki/File:StateLibQld_1_113968_Construction_of_a_new_infant%27s_school_at_St._Vincent%27s_Orphanage%2C_Nudgee%2C_1906.jpg*

[13] https://commons.wikimedia.org/wiki/File:Carlisle_Indian_School%2C_Carlisle%2C_Pa._Classroom_scene_LCCN2008675516.jpg

[14] https://commons.wikimedia.org/wiki/File:Hobo_sitting_on_a_fence%2C_ca.1920_%28CHS-1428%29.jpg

[15] Infrogmation, CC BY 2.5 <https://creativecommons.org/licenses/by/2.5>, via Wikimedia Commons https://commons.wikimedia.org/wiki/File:HoboMarkingsCanalStFerryCropped.jpg

[16] https://commons.wikimedia.org/wiki/File:ThreeHobosChicago1929.jpg

[17] https://commons.wikimedia.org/wiki/File:Unemployed_men_queued_outside_a_depression_soup_kitchen_opened_in_Chicago_by_Al_Capone%2C_02-1931_-_NARA_-_541927_%28cropped%29.jpg

[18] Frederick John Skill The Illustrated London News, CC BY 4.0 <https://creativecommons.org/licenses/by/4.0>, via Wikimedia Commons https://commons.wikimedia.org/wiki/File:A_soup_kitchen_Wellcome_L0000922.jpg

[19] https://commons.wikimedia.org/wiki/File:MontrealSoupKitchen1931.jpg

[20] https://commons.wikimedia.org/wiki/File:U.S._Capitol_on_the_arrival_of_a_bonus_petition.jpg

[21] https://commons.wikimedia.org/wiki/File:-50_B.E.F._Camp_Anacostia_D.C.%2C_D.C_%2732_LCCN2016827053_%28cropped%29.jpg

[22] https://commons.wikimedia.org/wiki/File:Shacks%2C_put_up_by_the_Bonus_Army_on_the_Anacostia_flats%2C_Washington%2C_DC%2C_burning_after_the_battle_with_the_military%2C_193_-_NARA_-_531102.jpg

[23] Seattle Municipal Archives, CC BY 2.0 <https://creativecommons.org/licenses/by/2.0>, via Wikimedia Commons https://commons.wikimedia.org/wiki/File:Hooverville_on_the_Seattle_tideflats%2C_1933_%2850495168952%29.jpg

[24] Hmalcolm03, CC BY-SA 4.0 <https://creativecommons.org/licenses/by-sa/4.0>, via Wikimedia Commons https://commons.wikimedia.org/wiki/File:Hooverville.jpg.webp

[25] https://commons.wikimedia.org/wiki/File:Interior_of_school_on_Mileston_Plantation%3B_School_begins_ver..._%283109740315%29.jpg

[26] https://commons.wikimedia.org/wiki/File:Couple-with-radio-and-Social-Justice-Michigan-1939.jpg

[27] https://commons.wikimedia.org/wiki/File:FDR-March-12-1933_%281%29.jpg

www.ingramcontent.com/pod-product-compliance
Lightning Source LLC
Chambersburg PA
CBHW071541120626
46550CB00006B/2531

* 9 7 9 8 8 9 2 9 6 4 2 1 0 *